Animal Kingdom Origami

Make Origami
MAMMALS

by Ruth Owen

PowerKiDS
press.

New York

Published in 2018 by **The Rosen Publishing Group, Inc.**
29 East 21st Street, New York, NY 10010

CATALOGING-IN-PUBLICATION DATA
Names: Owen, Ruth.
Title: Make origami mammals / Ruth Owen.
Description: New York : PowerKids Press, 2018. | Series: Animal kingdom origami |
    Includes index.
Identifiers: ISBN 9781499433555 (pbk.) | ISBN 9781499433494 (library bound) |
    ISBN 9781499433371 (6 pack)
Subjects: LCSH: Origami--Juvenile literature. | Mammals--Juvenile literature.
Classification: LCC TT872.5 O94 2018 | DDC 736'.982--dc23

First Edition

Produced for Rosen by Ruth Owen Books

Designer: Emma Randall
Photo Credits: Courtesy of Ruby Tuesday Books and Shutterstock.

Manufactured in the United States of America
CPSIA Compliance Information: Batch BS17PK: For Further Information contact Rosen Publishing, New York, New York at 1-800-237-9932.

Contents

What Is a Mammal?

There are more than 5,400 different **species**, or types, of mammals. They range in size from tiny bats, weighing less than an ounce, to the blue whale, the largest mammal on Earth. An adult blue whale can weigh 150 tons (136 tonnes)—that's the same as 30 elephants!

Mammals have four main characteristics.

Mammals are **vertebrates**, which means they have a spine, or backbone.

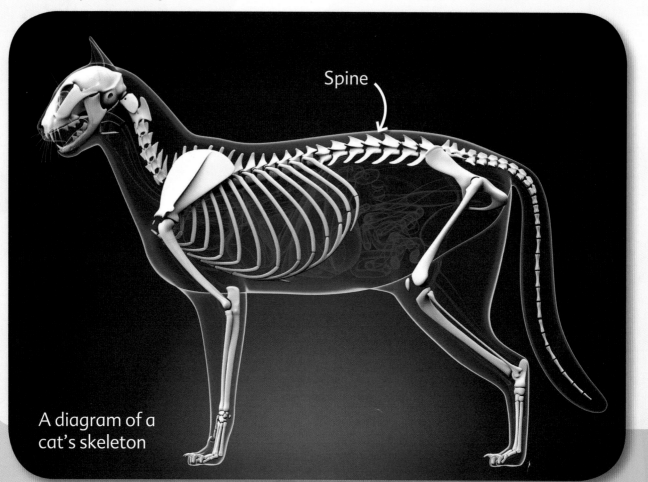

Spine

A diagram of a cat's skeleton

Mammals are **endothermic**, or warm-blooded. This means a mammal's body is able to **regulate** its inner body temperature. Even if an animal's environment is very hot or cold, its inner body temperature stays the same.

Arctic foxes are mammals that survive in temperatures colder than a freezer!

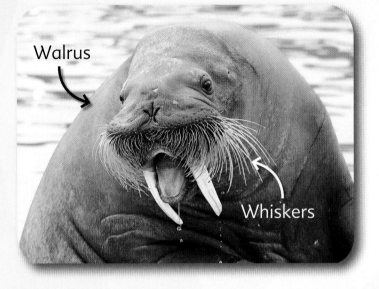

Walrus

Whiskers

All mammals have hair, fur, or wool. Some mammals don't have lots of hair—just a few bristles or whiskers.

All female mammals produce milk to feed to their babies.

A zebra foal drinking milk from its mother

Ready to discover more about mammals? Then grab some origami paper and let's get folding and learning all about mammals!

Polar Bears: Adapting to Cold

Polar bears are mammals with large, furry bodies that are perfectly **adapted** for life in one of the most extreme places on Earth. In the polar bear's Arctic home, winter temperatures may plunge to -50 °F (-46 °C) for weeks at a time. To keep it from losing heat, a polar bear has a **dense** coat of underfur covered by an outer layer of long guard hairs.

When hunting for seals, polar bears swim in the icy ocean. To protect them from the freezing water they have a thick layer of fat under their fur. This protective fat layer can measure up to 4.5 inches (11 cm) thick.

FOLD A POLAR BEAR

You will need:
- *A square piece of white paper*
- *A black marker*
- *Scissors*

Step 1:

Fold the paper in half, crease, and then unfold. Fold the paper in half in the opposite direction, crease, and then unfold.

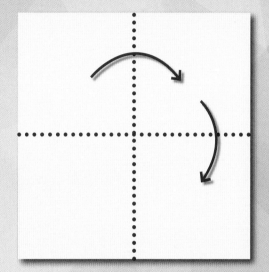

Step 2:

Fold the paper in half diagonally, and crease.

Step 3:

Fold the right-hand edge of the model back along the dotted line, and crease well.

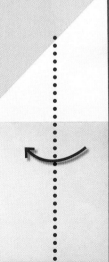

Step 4:

Now open out the fold you've just made.

Step 5:

Next, gently squash down and flatten the open section of the model to form the polar bear's head and legs.

Gently squash down and flatten here

Head

Front legs

Step 6:

To shape the polar bear's backside, fold in the left-hand point of the model along the dotted line.

Left-hand point

8

Step 7:

Now unfold and open out your model. Using the crease you made in step 6, reverse fold the left-hand point so that it is inside the model.

Step 8:

Then close up your model again.

Step 9:

To complete your polar bear model, use a marker to draw on ears, eyes, and a nose. You can trim the bottom corners of the legs, too, to create paws.

Step 10:

To make a polar bear cub, use a square piece of white paper that's one quarter the size of the main model.

Model opened out

Left-hand point of model

Elephants: A Very Handy Trunk

Elephants are the biggest animals that live on land. One of their most outstanding features are their long trunks. Elephants use these body parts for smelling, touching, gathering fruit, grass, and leaves, and for sucking up water.

An elephant's trunk can hold 2 gallons (9 liters) of water. It uses its trunk to squirt water into its mouth for drinking and to spray it over its back for a cooling shower. Scientists believe an elephant's trunk might be able to smell water up to 12 miles (19 km) away. A trunk can even be used like a snorkel for breathing when walking through deep water!

FOLD AN ELEPHANT

You will need:
- Two squares of paper in your choice of color
- Tape or a glue stick
- A black marker

Step 1:

To make the elephant's head, fold one piece of paper in half diagonally, crease, and then unfold. Fold in the opposite direction, crease, and unfold.

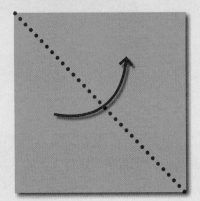

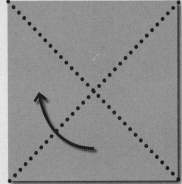

Step 2:

Fold down one point of the model so it meets the center line, and crease hard.

Step 3:

Fold up the point at the bottom of the model just a tiny amount.

Step 4:

Next fold in the two sides of the model along the dotted lines.

Step 5:

Now fold back the two sides of the model along the dotted lines, and crease hard. This will create your elephant's ears.

Step 6:

Turn the model over. To create the elephant's wrinkled trunk, fold up the bottom section of the model and crease hard.

Step 7:

Next, fold the trunk back down again, creating a small pleat. Crease hard.

Keep folding the trunk up and then back down again until the whole trunk is folded, or pleated, like an accordion.

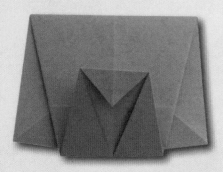

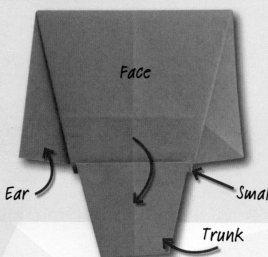

Face

Ear

Small pleat

Trunk

Step 8:

Unfold the pleated section of the model and your elephant should now have a wrinkled trunk!

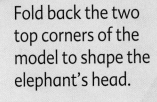

Fold back the two top corners of the model to shape the elephant's head.

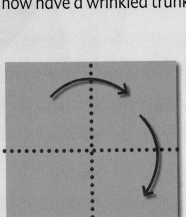

Step 9:

To make the elephant's body, fold the second piece of paper in half, crease, and unfold. Repeat in the opposite direction.

Step 10:

Now fold up a small section at the bottom of the paper and crease hard.

Step 11:

Turn the model over and fold both sides into the center. Crease hard.

Elephant's feet

Step 12:

Finally glue the elephant's head to the body.

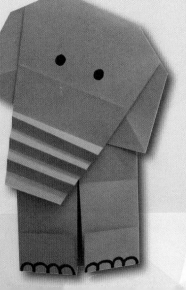

Draw on two eyes and give your elephant's feet some toenails. Your origami elephant is complete!

Lions: Top Predators

Some mammals, such as elephants, are plant-eating **herbivores**. Others, such as lions, are meat-eating **carnivores**. Animals that eat meat and plants, such as bears, are **omnivores**.

Lions are apex, or top, **predators**. This means they hunt many of the animals that live in their grassland or forest homes, but no animals hunt and eat lions.

Lions live and hunt in family groups called prides. Working as a team, these powerful hunters can catch large **prey**, including buffalo, giraffes, and even young elephants. Lions also hunt zebra, wildebeest, antelope, and warthogs.

FOLD A LION

You will need:
• A square piece of yellow or orange paper with one colored side and one white side
• A black marker

Step 1:

Place the paper colored side down. Fold in half diagonally, and crease.

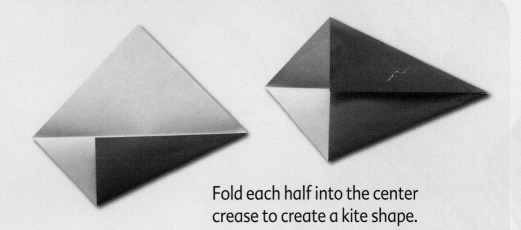

Fold each half into the center crease to create a kite shape.

Step 2:

Now open out each folded side in turn and fold a small sliver of the paper behind.

Step 3:

Turn the model over and make two folds as shown. Crease well.

Step 4:

Fold point B up to meet point A, and crease well.

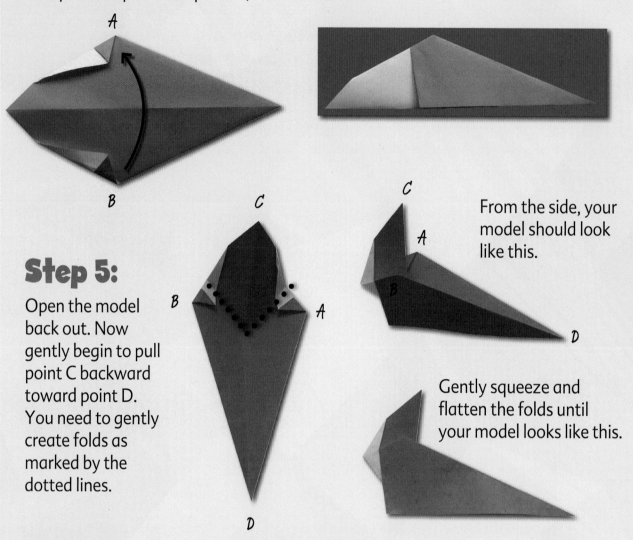

Step 5:

Open the model back out. Now gently begin to pull point C backward toward point D. You need to gently create folds as marked by the dotted lines.

From the side, your model should look like this.

Gently squeeze and flatten the folds until your model looks like this.

Step 6:

Now take hold of point E and open out the model.

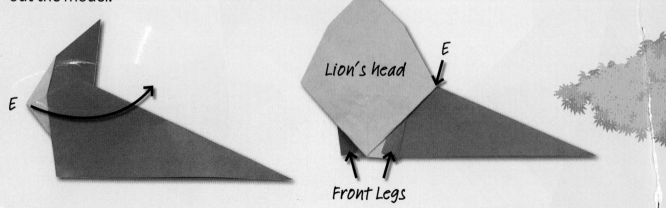

Lion's head

Front Legs

Step 7:

Fold down the top of the head to create the lion's face. Then tuck the bottom point of the face behind to create the lion's chin.

Step 8:

Fold the right-hand point of the model across the lion's body and face.

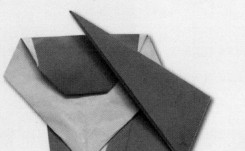

Step 9:

Then fold the point down to create the lion's tail.

Step 10:

Finally, pull out the tail and add a final fold to help steady the lion. Use the marker to draw on eyes, a nose, and whiskers.

Your origami apex predator is complete!

Dolphins: Water Mammals

Dolphins belong to an animal group called cetaceans. This group includes whales, dolphins, and porpoises. Cetaceans are mammals that live all of their lives in water. Like all mammals, dolphins have to breathe air. They breathe by swimming up to the water's surface and then taking in air through the blowhole on top of their heads.

Dolphins are born underwater. They are normally born tail first. Once a calf's head leaves its mother's body, the calf must start to breathe air or it will drown. A mother dolphin pushes her calf to the surface so it can take its first breath.

Blowhole

FOLD A DOLPHIN

You will need:
• A square piece of blue or gray paper
• A black marker

Step 1:

Place the paper colored side down, then fold in half and crease.

Step 2:

Fold the right-hand point of the model into the center, and crease.

Turn the model over, and fold the new right-hand point of the model into the center, and crease.

Step 3:

Now slide your fingers into the center "pocket" of the model. Gently open out the pocket to form a beak-like shape, then squash the model flat to create a triangle.

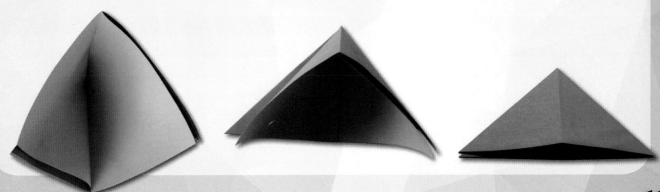

19

Step 4:

Now take hold of the top layer of paper on the right-hand side of the triangle and fold the point into the center. Crease well, and then unfold.

Step 5:

Take hold of the top layer of paper on the left-hand side and make a fold that follows the line of the crease you made in step 4. Crease well, and then unfold.

Crease made in step 4

Step 6:

Take hold of the top layer of paper on the left-hand side and make a new fold, this time following the line of the crease you made in step 5.

Crease made in step 5

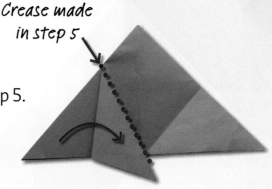

Step 7:

Now make a small fold along the dotted line and crease well.

Step 8:

Now fold down the top half of the model along the dotted line.

Your model should look like this.

Step 9:

Now fold the center point of the model upward along the dotted line.

Step 10:

Next, fold the left-hand top edge of the model down along the dotted line, and crease well.

Step 11:

Turn the model over. To make the dolphin's tail, take hold of the left-hand point of the model and fold it down and inward as shown.

The tail should look like this.

Next, fold the tip of the tail upward again. The tip will be made of two separate points of paper. Open out the two points to create the dolphin's tail flukes.

Step 12:

To make the dolphin's snout, fold the right-hand point back behind the model, and crease. Then fold the point back toward the right again, creating a small pleat.

Dorsal fin

Fold the point of the snout behind the model to give the snout a flat end.

Using a marker, draw on an eye.

Tail flukes

Flipper

Pleat

Orangutans: Learning from Mom

Orangutans are very smart mammals. However, just like human babies, young orangutans are helpless. They need their mothers to care for them and teach them everything they need to know. To get ready for their adult lives, young orangutans live with their mothers until they are about nine years old.

A mother orangutan teaches her baby how to climb through the rain forest trees. She also shows her baby which fruits are good to eat and where to find them. A female orangutan may only raise three babies in her whole lifetime. This is the lowest **birthrate** of any mammal.

FOLD AN ORANGUTAN

You will need:
- A square piece of orange paper
- A black marker
- Scissors

Step 1:

Fold the paper in half, and crease.

Fold in half again, and crease.

Step 2:

Now open up the top layer of paper to create a pocket.

Pocket

Gently squash down the pocket to form a square.

Step 3:

Turn the model over. Open up the triangle-shaped section of the model to create a pocket.

Open out here

Gently squash down the pocket to form a square.

Step 4:

Fold in the left- and right-hand sides of the model along the dotted lines, and crease. You should only be folding the top layer of paper.

Step 5:

Fold down the top point of the model, and crease.

Step 6:

Now open out the folds you made in steps 4 and 5. Lift up the top layer of paper to create a pocket.

Take hold of the top point of the pocket and pull it backward while gently squashing and flattening the sides of the pocket inward to create a diamond shape.

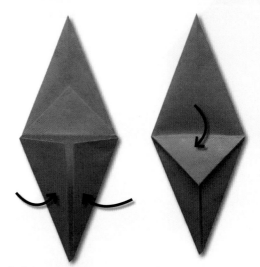

Top point

Top point

Pocket

Step 7:

Turn the model over. Fold in both side points, and crease well. Then fold down the small triangular flap in the center of the model.

Next, open out the three folds you've just made to create a pocket (as you did in step 6). Take hold of the top point of the pocket and pull it backward while gently squashing and flattening the sides of the pocket to create a diamond shape.

Your model should now look like this.

Step 8:

Fold the two side points of the model into the center along the dotted lines. You should only be folding the top layer of paper.

Step 9:

Turn the model over and repeat step 8. Then rotate the model by 180 degrees.

Your model should now look like this.

Step 10:

To make the orangutan's head, fold up the bottom flap of the model. Cut off the pointed end of the flap along the dotted line. Then fold the edges of the forehead and chin behind to shape the head.

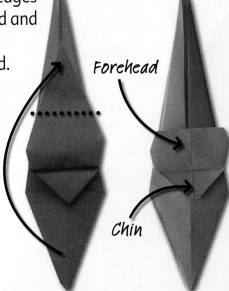

Forehead

Chin

Step 11:

To make the orangutan's arms, fold over one of the top points and crease hard. Then unfold, open out the arm, and fold it inside out using the crease you've just made. Fold the tip of the arm to make a hand.

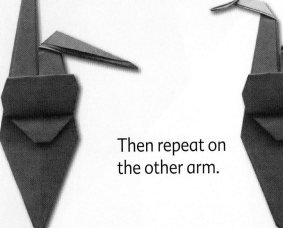

Then repeat on the other arm.

Step 12:

To make the orangutan's legs, make a short cut up the bottom point of the model. Fold the two points outward to create the orangutan's feet.

Step 13:

Draw on the orangutan's face with the marker.

Your origami orangutan is complete!

Bats: The Flying Mammals

Bats are the only type of mammal that can fly. Their wings are made of skin that's stretched between their front legs and their bodies. Like other mammals, they have hair or fur on their bodies.

There are more than 1,200 different species of bats. Many types of bats take flight at night to catch and eat flying insects. Others feed on fruit or drink nectar from flowers. Vampire bats actually feed on the blood of other mammals, such as horses or cows. A vampire bat makes a small cut in the skin of a sleeping animal using its razor-sharp teeth. Then it laps up a meal of blood from the cut!

FOLD A BAT

You will need:
- A square piece of paper in your choice of color
- Peel-and-stick goggly eyes
- Scissors

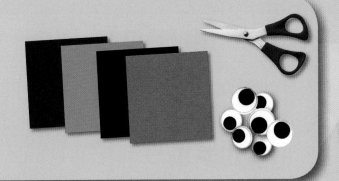

STEP 1:
Fold the paper in half diagonally, and crease.

STEP 2:
Unfold the paper and fold in half diagonally the other way, and crease.

STEP 3:
Fold the long side of the triangle over toward you, and crease.

STEP 4:
Now you'll begin to make the bat's wings. Fold one side in along the dotted line.

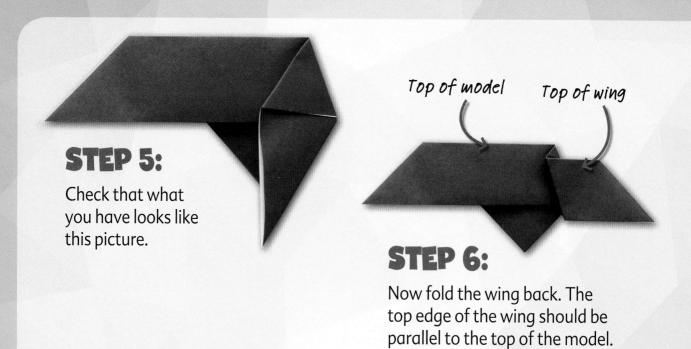

STEP 5:

Check that what you have looks like this picture.

Top of model   Top of wing

STEP 6:

Now fold the wing back. The top edge of the wing should be parallel to the top of the model.

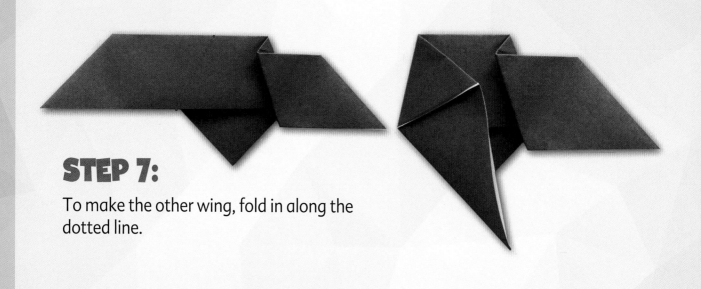

STEP 7:

To make the other wing, fold in along the dotted line.

STEP 8:

Now fold the wing back. Keep the top edge of the wing parallel to the top of the model.

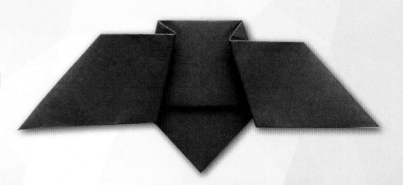

Ear   Ear

STEP 9:

Now, to make the bat's ears, use the scissors to cut along the dotted line on the bat's head.

STEP 10:

You can add eyes to your bat if you wish. Peel-and-stick goggly eyes can be bought from craft stores or from online craft suppliers.

Glossary

adapted
Changed physically over time to make it possible to survive in a particular environment.

birthrate
The number of births in a year or average lifetime.

carnivores
Animals that eat only meat.

dense
Compact or close together. A dense coat of fur has lots of hairs growing close together.

endothermic
Warm-blooded and able to maintain a constant inner body temperature.

herbivores
Animals that eat only plants.

omnivores
Animals that eat meat and plants.

predators
Animals that hunt and kill other animals for food.

prey
An animal that is hunted by another animal as food.

regulate
To adjust the temperature up or down to keep it at the same level.

species
One type of living thing. The members of a species look alike and can produce young together.

vertebrates
Animals with spines, or backbones, and a skeleton of other bones.

Websites

Due to the changing nature of internet links, PowerKids Press has developed an online list of websites related to the subject of this book. This site is updated regularly. Please use this link to access the list:

www.powerkidslinks.com/ako/mammals

Index